KT-154-642

The City of
GLASGOW

First published in Great Britain in 1994 for

Lomond Books
36 West Shore Road
Granton
Edinburgh EH5 1QD

Copyright © Colin Baxter 1994
All Rights reserved

No part of this book may be reproduced, stored
in a retrieval system, or transmitted by any means, electronic,
mechanical, photocopying, recording or otherwise, without
prior written permission of the publishers.

British Library Cataloguing in Publication Data
Baxter, Colin
Glasgow
I. Title
914.144304

ISBN 0–948661–51–8

Printed in Hong Kong

Front Cover Photograph: *BRIDGES OVER THE CLYDE*
Back Cover Photograph: *TENEMENTS, GREAT WESTERN ROAD*

The City of
GLASGOW

PHOTOGRAPHS BY
COLIN BAXTER

TEXT BY
JACK McLEAN

LOMOND BOOKS
EDINBURGH • SCOTLAND

CONTENTS

SECOND CITY OF EMPIRE

GLASGOW is, like all big cities, built in parts. And it is a big city; it prides itself on that. By the 1900s it was the second biggest city in Britain, the Second City of Empire, as one of Glasgow's chroniclers, Englishman but Glasgow immigrant Charles Oakley, described it in his seminal book (what else) *The Second City of Empire*. Oakley, now in his nineties, came here as a youth and stayed, became a Glaswegian – one with an outsider's view. Sometimes his view is a bit too clear for Glasgow folk. Sometimes he cannot penetrate the obfuscating fug of the curious culture which this most American of cities has thrown up over the years of its existence.

Take the last two statements, and take the last one first. The existence of Glasgow has not been real for much longer than 200 years. It started off as a geographical convenience – near a river – and an ideal place to kick off an ecclesiastical community with a cathedral founded in 1136 and a university in 1451. But the river came to mean more than religion ever would. Despite the fact that the surrounding areas were of little agricultural value, the river was. The Clyde could transport the produce of the rich land around itself, and when the mine owners and factory lords went into operation Glasgow was a perfect centre. By the mid-nineteenth century Glasgow had gone through a welter of commercial activity which stood it in good stead when it came to capitalist enterprise. The American tobacco trade had made it rich and splendid. (So had the spin-off, the slave trade, though Liverpool benefited more from that business.) The coal and steel and spinning trades had made Glasgow wealthy, and the focus was there not just for transporting goods but for manufacturing the final products too, so the city became a centre for industrial growth. It truly was the Second City of Empire. Perhaps the reason why Glasgow has always had a mote in its eye, a chip on its shoulder, is exactly that. Glasgow was Trade, in a way that Edinburgh, with its Assembly Rooms and Anglo-Scots aristos, was not. Glaswegians were wont to relish their lowly beginnings, and the massive Highland population, fresh from the Clearances, refused to dance to a far-off laird's tune. Democracy started early in Glasgow and has never left its streets of stone.

We will come back to that later. Ach, we'll come to it first. Glasgow's democracy is built into the stone of its buildings. When I suggest that it is an American city I know what I am talking about. *Herald* editor Arnold Kemp, writing a foreword to his paper's *Book of Glasgow*, and him an Edinburgh man of patrician background, was forced to write: "When I first came to Glasgow from Edinburgh – probably the biggest cultural switch any Scotsman may be required to make without going furth of the country . . ." he took a taxi and was asked if the restaurant he was looking for was at "Hope and Bath". An American notion – corner of third and . . .

True it is, as Kemp noted, that Glasgow is built in a grid pattern, like American cities, and true it is that the city has an American feel to its buildings. After all, the tenements which characterise Glasgow more than any other city in the world, were to be transported abroad as an idea for urban building, most strikingly in the big cities of the New World. Indeed, the first steel-frame buildings were originally built in Glasgow and the concept taken to Chicago by a Glasgow firm of architects, Burnett's, and the very first prefabricated cast-iron edifice (still there, Gardiner's Warehouse in Jamieson Street). But the population themselves were next door to Americans. "Give me your poor, your huddled . . . yearning to be free". Glasgow had its poor and huddled right enough, especially from the Highlands and Ireland. By the late days of the century it also had, to add to this explosive Celtic mix, Italian, Jewish (mostly from the Ukraine), Polish, Lithuanian, and other exotic communities. The last thirty years has seen the Asian communities seeping in, rather more slowly, and perhaps less dramatically than the foregoing, complying with what Glasgow expects as a process of assimilation, with the same curious ability as the other newcomers to merge into what is a very northern and rather bleak terrain, and stone from your very feet to as high as you can see.

A Yank would recognise it instantly. Oh, he would. The tenements; the squalor of some of them and the splendour of others. The poor and the huddled, and the bright glitter of the merchants and what has become the Merchant City, the huge mansions of the better off and the estates of the dispossessed, but most of all the enormous influence of the differing ethnic groups, the twelve thousand Italians, the eleven thousand Jews, the forty per cent of Glaswegians who can claim Irish descent, the Asian population now clambering up to nine per cent itself. The rest of us Highland, the middle class determined to spend their dosh on nice schools for their

BELMONT CRESCENT, KELVINBRIDGE
Glasgow from the air is often spectacular. Even in most built up
areas there is a green-ness which is unexpected.

BRIDGES OVER THE CLYDE
Glasgow has many bridges over the Clyde, all of them
necessary, but the latest of them, the Kingston Bridge, probably
more so than the others. These illuminated bridges add
much to the evening splendour of the city.

daughters, and more on their sons, the proletariat which votes Labour and vilifies its representatives because it knew them when their arse was out their trousers. Yes, an American city. Vitality and poverty and an ethnic mix. And a new city.

For Glasgow was undeniably new and had come from nowhere. As you look at the pictures – and Glasgow is horribly visual – throughout this book, you will see many pictures. The stories come out of them. Colin didn't choose Glasgow as some kind of random notion, but because he could get lots and lots of pictures. He's photographed Edinburgh before, and published many things on the amazing landscapes of Scotland. Why did he choose Glasgow? Because it intrigued him amazingly. It is the best preserved major Victorian city in the world, partly due to the inactivity of its largely East European style socialist city council, and partly due to a consciousness among its citizens that former glory should not be parcelled away readily.

Glaswegians themselves have a visual quality too which is a touch unique. They look like Glaswegians. You know what I mean. Glaswegians are not tall and by no means. They are Pictish and Celtic and Indo-European. You get plenty of wee guys and blondes and redheads and many may be black-haired Celts who came from Upper Scythia as in the Arbroath Declaration. In short, Glasgow is both very Scottish indeed and at the same time interwoven with other European and ethnic groups. Sounds like a cliché. Glasgow is a city of a cliché itself.

The city itself is built, as almost all cities are, out of a series of what were once villages. The older Gorbals chaps will tell you that Gorbals is quite separate from Hutchesontown, and Oatlands, and Kinning Park. People will tell you where Strathbungo is and why it is different from Govanhill. I live myself in Queen's Park and round the corner – I mean exactly round the corner – is Crosshill. A street away is Mount Florida.

The names signify small hamlets which once existed and indeed did so in living memory. People from Govan will tell you that it was once a Royal Burgh. People from Govan, over the age of forty anyway, refuse to be called Glaswegians: they are undeniably Govanites. Legendary street bookie, Corrie McGowan ("Don't be sorry, bet with Corrie") was such a Govanite he resented Glasgow Corporation demanding an application for a bookmaking licence when they made raffish bookies legal back in the early Sixties . . . He knew he was from Govan, no Glesca'. His son, Benny, a prominent lecturer in Economics, still maintains he is Govan and not Glasgow. Even more recently the denizens of Rutherglen are yet irritated at being part of the Upas Tree of Glasgow. They had their own burgh and their own town hall and their own councillors and their own identity. Sadly this has been taken away from them, but only in name. For a start Rug'glen inhabitants know they are actually in Lanarkshire, and retain a certain bucolic habit of mind.

Actually, Glasgow is to this day still a part of Lanarkshire. Even its centre of administration was, until thirty years ago, and in the middle of Glasgow itself, Ingram Street, just off George Square, called Lanarkshire House. Glasgow had greater notions and more pretensions and since 1888, with the erection of the quite astonishing City Chambers – a poem in porphyry, marble, and Edwardian smugness – the real seat of political power in this western city, this Second City of Empire, in this real capital of a nation, in this *real politik* of a country beleaguered by a lack of it, a positively Venetian show of grandeur. In this show and display Glasgow made itself a city state, and not a mere huddle of little town houses in what was once an agricultural countryside; since then Glasgow has known itself to be the Big City, the capital of Scotland.

Today Lanarkshire is an outlying district of Glasgow and so are Dumbartonshire, Renfrewshire, Ayrshire – all the shires which are around this dark mass. If it comes to that, so is every town and city of Scotland. If you need to stay in Scotland, you will eventually need to come to Glasgow. Dear old Glasgow town. There's nothing quite like it for it's going round and round. It still is. Even the bits that are in the country. Carmunnock and Cathcart would pass for the Cotswolds, for heaven's sake, but they are in Glasgow and, no matter how rural they may seem, are Glaswegian all the same. No matter how much you see Glasgow as entirely urban, you are also surprised to see how much countryside is in it. Glasgow as working-class? You will see a solid and handsome middle class – Glasgow's bourgeoisie might be less smug and anglified and complacent and sophisticated than that of other cities, but one thing is certain. You will see more grandeur in the stone-built piles of Dumbreck or Newlands or . . . or a large area of Glasgow in which the better off live, than you will in the grubby little suburbs of most other cities. I said you will see. Well Colin Baxter has seen, and photographed it, and you can see with your own eyes, for yourself.

FINNIESTON QUAY CRANE AT DUSK
Many artists have painted this icon, and quite rightly.
It surmounts the scene and at dusk possesses a positively
Florentine aesthetic quality.

GLASGOW COAT OF ARMS ON OLD GAS LAMP,
CATHEDRAL SQUARE
The Glasgow Coat of Arms is based on a quite charming legend of
the tree, the fish, the bell . . . Opposite: This vista, overlooking Dumbarton Road
and Partick in the west of the city, looks smoky, but since the Clean Air Act,
Glasgow has been a very smoke and fog free burgh indeed.

CLOSE, ROSE STREET, COWCADDENS

UPPER CLYDE CRANES AT DUSK
The cranes, once thick as bluebottles and damn near
seen from anywhere in the city, have gone. They now look
elegiac instead of forbidding. They now represent
empty hands too.

TENEMENTS

The beloved tenement of Glasgow is a little
different from elsewhere in Scottish towns and cities.
Often elaborate, (especially in the late Edwardian days), they are
integral to the Glaswegian aesthetic. Many post-war politicians
waged strong against the tenement, but Glaswegians
regard the buildings as their natural dwellings.

CANDLERIGGS
Despite the new proliferation of supermarkets
there are yet a large number of gaudy but nice exteriors.
This is in Candleriggs, where the old Fruit Market
continues to ply an ancient trade.

ST GEORGE'S CROSS
Once a new and grand example of Edwardian
architecture, this area which starts West End Glasgow
is now looked over by the high-rise flats
of the 60s and 70s.

GARNGAD & TOWNHEAD

Garngad (left) was hardly seen as new planning: it was
seen as emergency housing, and even more recently high-rise flats were
considered as a solution to the extremities of the Glasgow housing crisis.
The Townhead interchange, illustrated here from the air,
destroyed most of the old area and the district is
virtually unrecognisable today.

RIVER CLYDE

The Clyde River is the reason for Glasgow.
Widened much over the years it is still the metaphysical
artery of the city. Sadly it is virtually empty of life and certainly
industry today. The rowing clubs are glad of that and the
salmon have come back to the Clyde,
but the employment hasn't.

THE CITY CENTRE

The city centre is still the centre of this city. I was brought up in Townhead, opposite the Cathedral, next door to the Barony Church, just yards away from the The Royal Infirmary where Sir Joseph Lister (who unbelievably died as late as 1912) founded one of the greatest developments of modern medicine and surgery, antiseptics. I grew up in this pestilential area of a city, then of a million people. The second largest city in Britain at the time. The slums were dank and dark. The Clean Air Act was not then in force, and fog and smog curled round the blackened tenements like fur. There were no trees in the district, save for a few gaunt affairs in Cathedral Square. Poverty was life and post-war austerity made it seem more glum, less gaudy, more despairing even than the hopelessness of Depression Glasgow had been. Worse was to come.

The diaspora of the slum dwellers into the estates – the schemes – which came to ring the city, produced a new underclass. Ruchazie scheme I remember, because the children who were sent there, like wartime evacuees, were sent back to their old school in Townhead, my school where my father was the school janitor, miles and miles away. None of the schemes had schools. Or churches, or libraries, or pubs, shops, or transport. It was the greatest mistake Glasgow ever made, and has blighted the city ever since. The other mistake was allowing the old areas to rot and that certainly occurred in the oldest, the original, part of town, in "Toonheid". The powers that be set about knocking much of it down, leaving the dark, looming, Cathedral, the Provand's Lordship (the oldest House in Glasgow), and a set of municipal buildings like a workhouse out of Dickens. Today much of Townhead has been razed to the ground. The very first demolitions in the heart of the city were in Richmond Street, a row of fine Georgian buildings. One of them, I recollect, was used by the Cruelty People – the Royal Society for the Protection of Children. Another mansion housed three doctors, one of whom used half of it for his own residence. The Royal College of Technology (later to be known as Strathclyde University) owned two more of these astonishing buildings. They were demolished simply because the philistine city fathers saw anything old as an affront to New Socialism, and Georgian was older than they understood. They'd have pulled down the Cathedral if they'd been allowed to, as their Presbyterian forefathers had done before.

But the old city had a resilience one might not have expected. They might have turned much of Townhead into wasteground and then a motorway, but there were bits which did not turn to dust so easily. The High Street, when I was a boy, had one side with inside lavatories and the other without. Today both sides can comfort themselves with comfort. There are even inside baths. In my childhood you took your turn at the Toonhead Baths to scrub yourselves with carbolic soap, and ten minutes in the tub was all you had. It was hardly Joan Collins in soapsuds. Further down, nearer the Calton district, became the Merchant City. This was a grandiose idea of the 1980s but rational all the same. The area of the original Tobacco Lords was revitalised; the yuppies moved in. Splendid flats – for flat dwelling became once again fashionable – were created, with security entrances and ornate cortile. New sorts of Tobacco Lords, this time the professional classes, law, accountancy, media, computing, entrepreneurialism, combined with a touch of traditional Glaswegian spivvery, flew into the fastnesses of decent wealth. Glasgow has never gone for excessive show, only vulgarity, and it didn't when money started to flow into its oldest, worst, slummiest area. The result has been startling. Take yourself round the shops, where you will find restaurants like the City Merchant; a bar/restaurant/hotel/cafe like Babbity Bowsters in the centre of the new Merchant City would have appeared impossible fifteen years ago. The Italian Centre in Ingram Street? You must be joking.

But from this renaissance we have to go further geographically. Into the hub of the commercial centre. Once it was that Sauchiehall Street was the main artery. Hasn't been in years. Music hall and cinema were wont to refer to Sauchiehall Street as the very nub of Glasgow. The joke was that a big Highland polis once found a dead horse in Sauchiehall Street and dragged its bulk all the way into Bath Street for the simple reason that he couldn't spell Sauchiehall Street in his report. Today the top street in Glasgow is Buchanan Street. It insinuates itself betwixt the proletarian Argyle Street, where the plain people meet, and perhaps finishes, as fashionable at any rate, at St Vincent Street. This is expensive country and foreign visitors love it. Look above your head in this street and you will perceive an enormous and astonishing amount of ornament in stone. In fact, as every sensible Glaswegian knows to tell every

CITY CENTRE·CROSSROADS

A famous junction, photographed since Daguerre's time;
the crossroads of Argyle Street, Union Street and Jamaica Street.
The same junction has seen generations of Glaswegians, from men in
toppers and ladies in bustles, to boys in baseball caps and girls
in leggings. Truth to tell they don't look much different
really, and one suspects, aren't.

THE HIGH STREET

The High Street looking down to Glasgow Cross,
sometimes known as the Mercat Cross. You are looking down
a street which once housed the University of Glasgow, the fourth oldest
university in Britain and one of the oldest in the world. For many
years the former University site was inhabited by banana merchants.
Glaswegians saw this as worthy and fitting.

sensible visitor, in Glasgow, to look up anyway: you will be amazed. City centre Glasgow, commercial centre Glasgow, is redolent of Edwardian success, and after decades of failure, it is going back to its great days.

When I was a child the city centre had shops, department stores, strange byways of commerce, pubs, restaurants, coffee shops, tea rooms, establishments belonging to an earlier age. Most of the great industrial cities had such but Glasgow clung to them longer. I even worked in a city centre coffee house, the last in Glasgow. George Murray Frame was the name. Generations of Frames. Sadly, the last George Murray died a couple of years back. The house sold tobacco and was probably the very last link with the trade which had created Glasgow's original wealth. You cannot believe how much business was done by business in those days. And certainly in the coffee shops. There was Langs – the first ever self-service restaurant in the world (got turned into a designer bar in the early Seventies and never recovered) and the high tea places like Miss Buick's and Wendy's and the Thorn Tree in Dundas Street, and, oh so many. So much business to be done.

Much of it involved ships, shipbuilding, heavy industry, the locomotive industry in Springburn. Until the early 1960s three-quarters of the world's working locomotives had a Springburn plate on them. As a child in Townhead I played with the sons and daughters of this labour aristocracy: the Springburn railway industry was to be wiped out and closed down within five years but we were not to know the closure of industry itself was imminent or what it would mean to Clydeside. Oddly enough even the better off working-class people in places were financially poorer in the early fifties than they were twenty years later, but they felt wealthier than they do now. It was something to do with knowing who you were and living next door to your mum, uncle, relations and the friends you had grown up with. If this sounds somehow sentimental I cannae help it.

The proliferation of heavy industry brought about considerable prosperity, and enough of it to produce the unique architecture of Glasgow itself, North and South, East and West. Much of the reason why Glasgow preserved much of this uniqueness was because the city allowed itself to become so horribly impoverished during the recessions after the boom times that it couldn't even afford to knock its Victorian piles down. Heavens, it did its best to destroy the splendour of it all but so much had been built that so much was left. And the old Townhead, and the city centre, left enough, especially the old town centre. But there were other parts.

We have said that Glasgow, like all cities, is built in parts. There are four in essence. There is the West End, the East End, the South Side, and the Schemes. We will come to the Schemes last. But the West End first. And the reason for that is that the West End is the cultural artery of the place, always has been. Resentful sometimes the denizens of other parts of Glasgow have been. The University – Glasgow University that is, that old humphy-backed edifice with a spire like a swan's neck, is of recent date. And yet the university itself had first been built in the old Townhead, in the High Street before it moved to Gilmorehill up West. The University, the biggest in Britain in 1700, with over 400 students, started up where Glasgow began. And where Glasgow began has conducted the tenor and rhythm of the city ever since. It has never lost its beginnings from the cluster of cottages around the cathedral.

Today Townhead has a bereft look, with much of the area changed to motorway and wasteland. The new Cathedral complex includes rather a monster of an edifice, the so-called Museum of Religion. The Barony Church is still there, now a part of Strathclyde University and used for graduation ceremonies. Opposite is the statue of Prince William of Orange – King Billy. It had been removed early days to Cathedral Square and two splendid aspects of this equestrian stooky remain in the Glaswegian mind. One: the tail of the big white horse is organised on a ballcock, as a result of which it waves in high winds, a delight to all locals. The other is, that in the days when I was a child, the Orange Order, then but not now a powerful force in Glasgow, was wont to walk past the statue every year, and (the Glasgow gendarmerie never found out how it was done) the horse of the Dutch-born King of the United Kingdom was always painted stealthily in the night with green and white hoops, the livery of Celtic Football Club and the very antithesis of the philosophy of the Orange and Protestant community. Most "Toonheid" citizens, regardless of the religious divide which for many years had riven Scotland's city, thought of the prank as a glorious ex-ample of working-class humour. In the blackness of Townhead humour was needed. The earliest past of this city might well have been at the margin of city centre wealth and conspicuous consumption, but in the Townhead of early days, and even mine, the word consumption had an entirely different meaning from my economic one.

THE CITY CHAMBERS AND GEORGE SQUARE

CENTRAL HOTEL

RENFIELD STREET
The hub, really of Glasgow, since the demise
of Sauchiehall Street.

CENTRAL STATION & ARGYLE STREET, CITY CENTRE
From this picture you might get a glimpse of what Glaswegians
themselves are nearly conscious of: there is a Florentine aspect to their city.
A huddle of dark houses. A cross between Florence and O'Henry's
New York, with a dreadful climate thrown in. Oh, and
Highlanders and Irish to make it go
with an erratic swing.

ARGYLL ARCADE

Perhaps the biggest *galleria* devoted to jewellery and
silversmithing in Europe. The jewellers range from the top of it to the
cheapskate, and every young love is to be found here mooning over
rings and the like. It once also housed the famous Clyde
Model Dockyard, a haven for small boys who wanted the
ultimate Hornby-Dublo train set.

ROYAL EXCHANGE SQUARE

OLD AND NEW
A reflection of the glories of sandstone
sculpture in the windows of a
new style of building.

QUEEN'S STREET STATION AND THE CITY CHAMBERS
The Chambers are even more magnificent inside, and an example of
Edwardian confidence if ever there was one. The Square itself contains
13 statues of Victorian worthies, a marmoreal splendour to us all, and has
held rock concerts, five-sided football, solemn commemorations of the last
two wars, and the raising of the Red Flag in 1916. It is, and remains,
the centre of Glasgow and seen as that by the lieges.

THE CITY CHAMBERS AND GEORGE SQUARE

THE WEST END

Winter is coming, the night is beastly derk
the erc lights are fizzing in the West End Perk;
All of the erc lights fizz like gingerade
End aih'm beneath your window
with this cherming serenade.

This musical ditty, popular for many years, but now long forgotten except by older folk and younger folk in traditional music pubs, sums up what was once a genuine divide in Glasgow, and visually too. For the West End was for toffs. What in Edinburgh was Morningside, with its exaggerated gentility, especially its accent, was replicated in Glasgow's West End Kelvinside. The accent itself, long since gone and forgotten in both cities except as practised by a handful of octogenarians, once characterised a sort of attitude which was hewn in street and stone. Dear God, the very buildings seemed to say: "Aih ehm middle-cless: youse are scruff". Kelvinside is now full of new immigrants, mostly from Asia, and students have filled up the flats which are now bedsits. The days of the top floor being the nursery and the basement a habitation for maids in flouncy lace petticoats, are long over. These town houses are flats now.

Yet it was not so long in the past that a celebration of money indeed existed. As a boy I found myself travelling about this town, working for the very tobacco company whose name you encountered earlier, George Murray Frame. It was my job, as a little lad, still at Allan Glen's School and only thirteen, travelling about Glasgow with great parcels under my arm, going to all the West End addresses, to deliver cigars, hand-made cigarettes with family monograms on each fag, newspapers and magazines, and, in the case of old Mr Murray Frame himself, ensconced in the wonderfully Art Deco Kelvin Court apartments, something out of an Ellery Queen novel of the Twenties – ice-cream, wrapped in his morning newspaper. Mr Murray Frame had a nurse, I remember, like something out of a Raymond Chandler novel.

Hillhead, now the land of Glasgow University students, was then a country beyond mine in Townhead. The flats were massive. I delivered to a composer who had a grand piano and his butler answered the door. These were the last days. The days when I was a young shaver the students had taken over, and I was one of them.

Strange, ancient women, widows whose income had long since gone, opened up the dark long houses to cheery and irresponsible young men and women, students and nurses, and even a few ne'er do wells who had left their parental homes out of a notion of independence. Hillhead was abandoned by the better off, and indeed, so was Kelvinside, the magnificent Park area, even the Great Western Road, and further along, in favour of easier, more suburban outreaches like Milngavie, Bearsden and further afield, out past the city boundaries. Today you will see the magnificence of these terraces and tenemental lands, blurred now by the presence of commercial companies.

Perhaps the Park area is most representative of what has happened to the West End. It is an inexplicably beautiful spread of architectural show; inexplicable because no single architect (though Galt comes to mind, a minor but effective designer of the late 1880s, whose son went on to produce fine buildings all over the South Side of the city) can be said to be entirely responsible for this amazing bit of planning. Like most cities, Glasgow is built upon seven, and perhaps more, hills, and certainly the Glasgow valley lent itself to an adornment of buildings one could not have grasped in a flatter plain. (Just take a look, as we will later, at the Garnethill area of Glasgow where the Rennie Mackintosh masterpiece of the School of Art lies.) And high above Sauchiehall Street on one side, and Woodlands Road on the other, is this piece of Victorian planning, worthy of Edinburgh's New Town – with less grace, but more vigour. The last thirty or forty years have seen it turned into a haven for accountancy firms, oil companies, financial organisations. These are the best of it. For many years little fly-by-night companies wormed in, allowing the premises to slowly fade, or occasionally throwing a fit of aesthetic lunacy, and painting the exteriors in puce or pink.

Certainly one of the most marvellous architectural spots of Europe, worthy of a Haussman, was reduced over three decades, and it will take decades more, and people with eyes in their heads, to restore it all. The New Glasgow Society, founded in 1963, pushed mightily to maintain, at a time when the municipal warlords were agog at the prospect of destroying anything which smacked of the old Victorian order and replacing the marmoreal piles with a vision straight out of East Berlin, the then unfashionable idea that Victorian and Edwardian Glasgow should be restored. They

HILLHEAD
Hillhead was once a highly prosperous area.
Today, many of its large flats are taken up by students at the nearby
University, but colourful reminders of its more
elegant past still remain.

SCOTSTOUN, VICTORIA PARK AND BROOMHILL
The sun glistens from the fenestration of the flats at dusk.
Most would prefer the douce
sandstone flats below.

concentrated on the Park Circus environs at first, and, though unsuccessful in bringing the residents back as well as the splendour, at least Park yet remains, wounded and battered, but still there. The Society has always concentrated its efforts on the West Side of the city and so tends to miss out on other parts. It most certainly missed out where the lower orders always worked and lived.

For the West End is the west side, and districts such as Anderston, Partick, Maryhill, Scotstoun, have an architectural heritage often ignored. Minerva Street in black Anderston, with its long round sweep of elegant tenement, housed until recently as much misery as you will find in Britain. It was the centre for the old National Assistance Board. Today it is again what it was once, a glory in sandstone. Recent years has seen the district a little, but a touch desultorily, yuppified. Actors John Cairney and Alana Stevenson lived there, and many a young theatrical bought their first houses in the nearby terraces. The Director of Education for Strathclyde – the largest local government post in Europe – Frank Pigniatelli, hails from Anderston and once suggested to his wife that they move back. She looked round her large and lovely garden in a splendid suburb and gave Frank's whim short shrift. Yet I know what Frank was talking about. He and I were once bus conductors together, thirty years ago, when Glasgow's bus conductors and clippies were the stuff of legend. I do not share his roseate view of the slums, but I have heard it from less sentimental men and women than Frank and I recognise it.

West End? Certainly. Byres Road and the Hillhead and University environs were heady stuff for generations of students from the Western Isles, or other parts of the Highlands, or Lanarkshire, or students from every part of Scotland even English provincials who might not have managed Oxford or Cambridge. Oh, the West End was heady stuff, as student areas always are. But we have already referred to other parts of the West. We talked of the money and merchant boys in the area.

Further in the west of the city were the better off. Every British city has its better off in the west, simply because the wind blows from west to east in Britain. Plague meant that everywhere in the British Isles the wealthy moved to the West; tried to avoid the winds of disease. It took more than a century for medical men to persuade the politicians and the rich that winds had nothing to do with it and that proper water supplies and sewerage facilities would mean that disease was conquerable. Took decades to persuade the rich that their own children were dying of the same neglect, the same avoidable circumstance, which the children of the poor were suffering from. In fact, Glasgow, early days, recognised it and built the best water supply ever, with a remarkable engineering feat – a supply from Loch Katrine. Crumbling as the sewerage system now is in Glasgow, it was so ahead of its time in Victorian days that it still is ahead. Every European city yet envies Glasgow, but much needs to be done and spent to update this wonder of Glasgow now.

The West part of the city incorporates the new old money. Here it is that the rather silly and ersatz Gothic University lies, old as it is. Here you will find the largest and most august collection of paintings and sculpture in Britain, outside of the Tate Gallery, in the Glasgow Art Gallery, Kelvingrove. The park in which it lies is a monument to late Victorian muscular Christianity. Frankly, the Glaswegians have never cared for either the philosophy or the park. The stark rigidity of Kelvingrove Park has never stirred the Celtic blood, and though for many decades Kelvingrove was a sort of parade for the better off and the children with their nannies, generally Glaswegians, of whatever class, have preferred to walk their weans and themselves in more pastoral vistas. A formal park may have seemed fine as a municipal notion, but the hankering for the heath, the hill, and the rough heather, lay deep in the city people who had originated in exactly that far away in Scotland. This is a fancy way of saying that Glaswegians liked open country, awffy like where they had come fae themselves.

But it is new old money. The old money came from overseas trade. The new coins into the coffers came from business in the city itself. All over Glasgow you will find this remarkable expansion of money, but no clearer picture can you find than in the outstanding prosperity of the west side of the city. We have talked of the mansions of Kelvinside and Great Western Road, the well-set town houses of Hillhead, the decent working-class aristocracy domiciles in Partick; all this was to change. The change was sudden and halfway through the last decades of the nineteenth century at that. And later, during the depression of the Thirties, the rich got less rich, but, Jesus, the poor got a great deal poorer indeed. And it changed the look of this complacent enclave to the west.

PARK CIRCUS, KELVINGROVE

CHARING CROSS MANSIONS

'WALLY' CLOSE, BYRES ROAD

Wally is the local dialect for ceramic. Many of the better
tenements had their closes clad in some quite beautiful tiles,
mostly made in Holland or Belgium and the Art Nouveau Movement
provided a wealth of decoration. A wally close was
undeniably a sign of wealth.

FISHMONGER, PARTICK

PARTICK IN THE RAIN
A spectacular rainscape – and heavens,
Glasgow is used to that – in Partick just before
the West End. Silver it looks, but dreich it is
when you are there yourself.

CLOSE, YORKHILL

Tenements are the way of dealing with Glasgow's
inhabitants. From the air, I may say, these tenements
off Great Western Road (opposite) look a lot more
orderly than the inhabitants ever
allowed them to be.

WOODLANDS ROAD AND LYNEDOCH STREET, CHARING CROSS

HUNTLY GARDENS, HILLHEAD

THE GLASGOW UNIVERSITY SPIRE ON A WINTER DUSK

KERSLAND STREET, HILLHEAD
Another example of doorway art. Too many people
have taken out the stained glass of yesteryear, but they have
undeniably regretted the decision. Opposite: The University Spire inspires
many a Gilmorehill student and indeed looks lovely, if a little
unreal. Down from its grassy slopes you will find the
students picknicking in the Spring.

KELVINGROVE MUSEUM AND ART GALLERY
Only the Tate in London has more visitors each year.
Kelvingrove is a fabulous museum in itself, with marvellous exhibits,
but it also possesses a magnificent collection of paintings and sculpture,
including a rarely-seen collection of pre-Raphaelite and Victorian
genre works. Opposite: Tenements and park: a common
sight in the *Dear Green Place*.

KELVINGROVE PARK AND YORKHILL

PARTICK, DOWANHILL AND HILLHEAD
West End of the city; the working-class bit. Just shows you
how close Glaswegians live to each other.

A SUMMER DAY IN HILLHEAD

EASTERN APPROACHES

Lots of money. The West End of Glasgow was the place for money, for and from the new and emergent middle class which Glasgow's industrial prosperity had thrown up. To go with such prosperity were schools such as Kelvinside Academy, Glasgow Academy, girls' schools such as Laurel Bank and Westbourne. The High Street was already there, in the west part of the city centre, but they founded a sister school for girls in the West. To this day the west of the city has a welter of institutions for the sons and daughters of the well off. But the other side – the East – has not. It is the poor relation.

In fact the East side is horribly conscious of this. Eastbank Academy, founded in 1894, celebrated its centenary with a highly self-conscious gala. Cliff Hanley, the Glasgow writer and novelist, went there, and boasts in the sort of way that people do when they are aware that nobody has heard of them. All the Eastbank people do. Elsewhere in Glasgow people don't have to boast of their schools, of their mansion houses or shopping areas, or anything really. In the east they know they are still peasants. And they were of course, and yet retain a difference from the rest of the city which belongs to an agricultural feeling which possesses the East Ender.

The East End starts near the city centre itself, just beyond Townhead and the Calton. Nobody knows why Dennistoun begins it all, but in the Glaswegian mind Dennistoun has never quite belonged to Glasgow. As a child I knew it as a flourishing area full of dentists and doctors and bank managers. Alexandra Parade had been in Edwardian days a highly fashionable area and it retained a somewhat shabby gentility right into the 1960s. A little further south though, were some of the roughest areas in Europe.

The Barras comes to mind. Barrowland was exactly that, a barrowland. Maggie McIvor was the lady who started off this remarkable market, Britain's version of the Paris flea market. Mrs McIvor was a fixture in Glasgow for over half a century. She wore buttoned boots even into the years of the Second World War, had one brown eye and one blue one, was illiterate, swore horribly, and had more financial nous than Rupert Murdoch and Nubar Gulbenkian put together. She would have made

John D. Rockefeller look like a wimp. When she died she was worth millions. For the Barras was exactly what poor Glaswegians, from Highland glen and Donegal bog, needed: cheap. It still is. It was where the proletariat bought their clothing, and their few pathetic luxuries. Bert and Barry's sold shoes here. The duo were patter merchants and supreme at their business. Used to bill themselves as "stars of wireless and film" because a few programmes and a wee short film had been made about them. I remember them well because my parents bought my shoes from them when we were poor, and the brogans were so ill-fitting (no Walk-Rite stuff then) that I have suffered from deformed toes ever since and still have pain if standing too long.

Today the Barras has changed but little. The barkers still operate their wiles upon a largely working-class audience (for the Barras is showbiz and the crowds know it). "I'm not asking three hundred and fifty quid for this Limoges dinner service; I'm not even asking two hundred and fifty green ones for this superb example of the French potter's craft; for this thirty-seven notes, all right then have it fur twenty, I'll throw you in a teapot, made by Eve Son Lorron himsel." Here you will find "girls' knickers, three for fifty pence", or "men's shirts, latest fashion, three for two quid". Everything comes in threes. Everything is cheap. Not much of it is any good. I know. I once sold jewellery at a stall here. Every week a customer would come up and complain that the lady's bracelet I'd sold him a fortnight back was turning his sweetheart's wrist green. "Whit d'ye expect fur thirty bob, ya cheapskate!" I would riposte, hoping my burly minder would come to the rescue. The Barras is cheap but not nasty, raffish and not respectable, but Glaswegians love it. A show it is, and no visitor should miss it on a Sunday morning.

But the East End extends further East. And further south, the East also has Bridgton – Brigton it is known as. This was the very area named, near as dammit, in the stereotypical Glasgow novel *No Mean City*, as the antagonist to Gorbals, a district we will come to later. Bridgton was where the famed street gang the "Billy Boys" hailed from. Their leader was called Billy Fullerton and I remember the crowds out in the streets at his funeral. A bit of a local hero.

At one time Fullerton commanded two thousand lumpen thugs in the streets and there were politicians who colluded with him in the Thirties: he was close to the British Union of Fascists. Characteristically, for a ned (the Glasgow word for thug), he

DENNISTOUN

THE BARRAS

Little did Maggie McIver, the rough and ready chatelaine
who founded this institution of the city, know that it would grow to be
one of the great bazaars of the western world. Every Glaswegian,
great or humble alike, harbours affection for
its own "flea market".

did not fight in the War. He claimed to be a conscientious objector, and even got away with that preposterous proposition. It is true and disgraceful that the government used him to infiltrate the Communist Party during the days of the Spanish Civil War. But Brigton was an area of Protestant ascendancy; it is not so now – it is poor. And next door to it is Parkhead, where the Celtic football team have their stadium. Celtic and Rangers football teams have played a major part in the psychological architecture of this city for over a century.

But perhaps Celtic has been a bigger player than the largely Protestant team on the South Side of Glasgow. Parkhead area itself is undistinguished; indeed the stadium is a byword for seediness in Scottish football. But Celtic Football Club holds a commitment from the Glasgow-Irish community which has had such a large part in the making of Glasgow. Sectarianism should have rooted itself in this city but it hasn't; you have to look to the rural areas of Ayrshire or Lanarkshire for that. Glasgow was industrial before all and the religious divide of my youth dissolved in the path of the disaster of the death of industry in the city.

Parkhead itself is a strange area, largely slum and park, but with a notion of what lies further in the East. East Enders know this and are oddly inarticulate about the phenomenon, even Cliff Hanley. For a start the inhabitants are poorer than anywhere else, but richer in their neighbours. The children are well dressed, but more of them go to prison. This is the traditional area for bright boys and girls to go agley. It is also a touch country. Robroyston, Riddrie, Shettleston: these are alien lands to city folk.

Robroyston is where William Wallace was captured in 1305, sent down to England and done to death by the perfidious Albions of the day. Oddly enough, Wallace, the greatest Scottish patriot of all time, was born just outside of Glasgow, in Elderslie. There are monuments to the hero in both Robroyston and Elderslie. Both areas are somewhat bucolic and the setting for nice big mansions and a few desultory farms. Any visitor to Glasgow will discover the oddness of being a quarter of an hour's drive from the city centre yet in the middle of countryside and history. Certainly neither Robroyston or Elderslie look like the proper spot for a conscience of a nation, but then Scotland, and certainly Glasgow, is like that. It has style but no class.

And there is no class at all about the East End, but there is lots of money. Some of the most stylish villains Glasgow can throw up – and that is a lot of style and villain – live in considerable splendour in massive detached houses here. East Enders know who they are, where they live, and they, being very perspicacious chaps indeed, know who you are, and where you live.

The sensible Glaswegian forgets that fact. And the East, the Far East, is yet a place which disturbs many Glaswegians. It is the road to the depths of Lanarkshire. On the way is Easterhouse, the biggest housing estate in Europe, a disaster invented by high-mindedness, and perhaps the greatest architectural error ever made in the world. Bigger than towns like Perth, housing a bigger population, it struck a chord in the tabloid press back in the Sixties, when an amnesty for weapons was choreographed by showbiz star Frankie Vaughn, aided, strangely by writer Archie Hind, whom you have encountered before in this book. Archie wrote the novel *The Dear Green Place*, and rediscovered the expression. (Glasghu is Gaelic for Dear Green Place). Easterhouse is now a byword, a little unjustifiably, for inner city deprivation. Drugs and deprivation are most certainly there, but it remains largely a decent community. Frankly, Easterhouse is really country.

And so is most of the East End. Starting with tenements it trails off to cottages. East Enders have never felt entirely at home in the streets of stone. Incidentally, the soft drink company, Barrs, whose product Irn Bru is ubiquitous in Scottish homes, has its factory in the East End. Wills cigarette factory was here too. So was Templeton's Carpet Factory, a splendid pastiche of the Doge's Palace in Venice, a wee bit of daftness in Glasgow Green. The Green also houses two major rowing clubs on the Clyde, the People's Palace which possesses memorabilia of Glasgow's past, a past some of the middle classes would prefer to forget. Until recently it was presided over by Elspeth King, removed from office as curator for her uncompromising stance over the proletarian nature of this strange city museum. And further to the East, past the big houses, past the Easterhouse estate, past the last vestiges of the city, is the Zoo. Calderpark, now Glasgow Zoo. Right on the outskirts. A sad place with caged wild animals. I do not come from the East End but to me the denizens have always seemed a bit wild, but caged at that.

PEOPLE'S PALACE

BUTCHER'S WINDOW
The high-rise flats (opposite) have overshadowed
the city, not least the old tenemental buildings.
This is sunset at the edge of Dennistoun
and Camlachie.

THE SOUTH SIDE

To a large number of Glaswegians, especially the older ones, the South Side, or "Soo-Side", means simply one district – Gorbals. In fact South Side Glasgow is the bulk of it, and it is quite different from the rest of the city, even quite different from any area of any city in the United Kingdom. It was ever the place for immigrants. Into the South Side fiefdoms came the Highland people, and then the Irish. The Jews came here, and the Polish, and the Italians. Gorbals, Hutchesontown, they were old areas. Once they held the wealthy, with big town houses, and wide streets like Portland Street. Then the Gorbals took in the clerks and managerial classes.

Gorbals bred such worthies as John Buchan, novelist, civil servant, later Baron Tweedsmuir, then Governor-General of Canada. Buchan was a former pupil of Hutcheson's Grammar School, the most academic of all schools in Glasgow. My own brother went there, in the Gorbals. Once, at a conference, he overheard English colleagues speak in awe of him. "He is one of the bosses", he heard them say, "and he went to school in the Gorbals!". A wee chuckle to himself. Sure, thirty-odd years ago Hutchie Grammar was in the Gorbals, but even then it was the very epicentre of scholastic and middle-class aspiration.

Truth to tell, the Gorbals had become myth. And the myth was quite unreasonable, meant nothing in reality. Enough damage has been done to Glasgow's image over the years, but Gorbals exemplified the place, and Gorbals was Glasgow. It was destroyed and pulled down many years back but the pall of the image has lain over the city for fifty years. Nobody, not even Glaswegians, seems to know that John Buchan lived here – even wrote a series of novels about "The Gorbals Diehards", young children brought up in a decent working-class area as it then was – nobody remembers The Gorbals' Hutchie Grammar, now a school set in another district of the South Side. Few know anything about the Gorbals at all any more, except the older people.

The area had originally been set aside for the managerial classess, the people who were needed to operate the new industries. Later the Highlanders and the Irish came and the factors began to split perfectly decent houses into single flats, single-ends, a room, a kitchen. The peasants who came knew little of city living and accepted the level of exploitation which they were offered, often by their own countrymen, and more often than not by their own countrywomen. Poverty was equally accepted, but Gorbals seemed, if very different from the background of the largely agricultural immigrants, a new but at least a shared experience.

Gorbals was eventually razed to the ground and the "New" Gorbals emerged. Today the area has no social focus of any kind at all, if you don't count the drugs scene. In the last few years the high-rise flats – notably the disasters created by award-winning architect Sir Basil Spence – have been pulled down. In a dreadful irony an onlooker was actually killed when one of the flats was demolished with explosives. If the old Gorbals was a wen of deprivation and despair, it was as nothing to the new Gorbals, and South Siders are angry at the replacement of an old and ordered and poverty-stricken area by a new, inchoate, and damn near mendicant community.

But the South Side was in fact larger than Gorbals, and a lot larger too. If you went further south you would come to Govanhill and Shawlands, Mount Florida, Pollockshields, Dumbreck, and to the west was Govan. Hampden Park, the national stadium was here. So were all these remarkable parks and parkland. Glasgow has more parkland per square mile than any other city in the world. And the South Side is where much of the green grass is. Captain George, of the Clyde helicopter firm, which does a tour every minute and every hour for tourists and Radio Clyde alike, describes Glasgow as "greener than Celtic Park, greener than Borneo. Just take a look at the South Side". I know what Captain George means. Outside my own window, overlooking Queen's Park, I know.

Queen's Park is thus called because Mary, Queen of Scots waited there, saw her army assemble by what is now Langside Monument, overlooking the south part of this piece of countryside in the middle of a city, and watched from what is now Linn Park, a space called Courtknowe, in the hill above Cathcart. Courtknowe is an ordinary little place for a royal pilgrimage. Near it is a small and long since worked-out quarry. A hundred yards away was Cathcart Castle, demolished, ludicrously, as recently as 1980. The park itself had at one time an open countryside appeal: a little wood, a river, bridges over it, a golf course, a waterfall, and by its edge the Snuffmill

GORBALS
The new Gorbals has been largely a disaster.
Today the city blows up the appalling "filing cabinets for people",
a memorable phrase of ex-political activist and current
broadcaster Jimmy Reid, and the populace is
glad to be rid of them.

GOVAN

It has never seen itself as Glasgow and Govanites
regard themselves as aristos, which in the days of the
Labour Aristocracy in the shipyards,
they rather were.

bridge. Twelve minutes from the city centre the little village and its park lay there, an opening for the city dweller. The local area, all around it was almost a company town, for most of the houses were owned by, and certainly everybody worked for, Weir's Works. To this day, Weir's owns much of the local area, and has a rather decent sports ground nearby where it runs a cricket team, and a sports day for the children of the employees.

A large amount of the rest of this area is owned by the Catholic Church, and even more of it by the Church of Scotland. There is a reason for this. The South Side was sold off for housing by both churches a century and more ago, but if you take a look around the Queen's Park, Strathbungo and Crosshill districts, among all the housing in its grand sandstone cladding, you will find more churches than almost anywhere else in Europe. Most of them are now closed and crumbling. But once the lower middle-classes took their various religions seriously and the result is a plethora of wonderful late-Victorian Gothic fantasies now long since descending into a redundant desuetude.

Down by Battlefield though, lies the South Queen's Park Synagogue. It was but a year back that they inaugurated the new stained glass windows, designed and created by an artist himself a gentile. It is not difficult for a Soo-Sider to understand such a measure from the Jewish Community. Such anti-semitism as has existed in Glasgow has never had much of a response in South Side. My own father, from Mull, but brought up in Gorbals, spoke Gaelic and Yiddish, and even English, and so did everybody else in that cauldron of immigrant poverty.

But the South Side was never snobbish, unlike the West of the city. It had wide streets. The sky was everywhere. Big skies in the South. I was brought up in Toonheid, but it was wonderful coming back to the South. The skies most of all were wonderful. The weather, it is said, is better here. And here in the South is where I am writing from. The smart people, the writers and artists and media people don't come from here, where I am, where I live. Further out from me is the edge of the city, over by. Netherlee lies just outside the boundary, and Clarkston. There are quiet little, and big, houses, and even bigger houses in Whitecraigs or Newton Mearns. The toffs live there: the women in pleated Jaeger skirts, schoolgirls in uniforms and schoolboys clad in military tunics, the men in pin-stripes, the lawns outside the big stone edifices dressed even more formally. Glasgow is a city full of working-class vitality, but run by the middle class and generally, run well. The South Side is an exemplar of it. Over to the west lies Govan, over to the east is Oatlands and beyond. Still in Glasgow is Cambuslang, almost country that is.

Things have changed much in the South Side – Asian families have created a home for themselves here, taking over from the successive generations of Highland, Irish, Jewish, Polish, Italian, incomers. So far they have had little social effect in comparison to their antecedents – to this day the South Side pub culture is largely Irish and the influence of the people from across the water is incalculable. The Asian peoples have had a smaller effect on Glasgow, though the Sikhs, because they permit themselves a libation or two in the pubs, have perhaps in their own way been influential in this particular part of Glasgow. The Pakistani and Islamic groups are very strong in the business sector and many leaders from those communities have made their presence felt in the last twenty years or so, but they have added very little in the development of the way Glasgow looks, tending to keep a low profile.

Certainly the Soo-Side, for all its large numbers of Asian immigrants (and bear in mind that any Asian under thirty-five is likely to have been born here) has not seen what I personally would like to see – a visual change, a touch of the Punjab, the bright colours of Bengal in the middle of the greyness of Glasgow. I would like to see regenerated the love of verve and colour among Celts and Europeans which came to life when the original Glasgow upsurge found the means and the confidence to make things happen. In the wide space of the South Side and among the greenery, and across the road from my house, in the middle of the park, I often see the bright saris, and the beautifully dressed little girls with their mamas swathed in the chador, on a sunny day under the chestnut trees: then it is I wish that Glasgow was always sunny, and that I had always lived (yes, I could bear to have missed out on the slums of my childhood) on the South Side. The South Side does that sort of thing to you.

CARDONALD

Cardonald was set up as a model housing scheme
and remains to this day rather well set up if a little shabby
due to the increasing age of the inhabitants. But you can
see how the planners saw it in its origins.

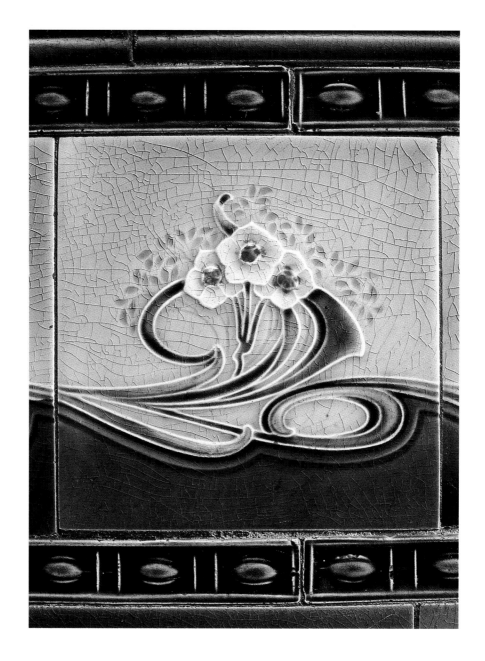

VICTORIA ROAD

The tenements in the South Side of Glasgow are
often large and roomy and richly decorated, especially in the
tiling and painting of the closes, even, indeed in the heavy stained glass
windows. These tiles in the late 1890s Victoria Road, show the
exquisite Dutch ceramic tiles which are redolent
of a decorative age.

GLASGOW ITSELF

Glasgow is a city of Victorian, and Edwardian, confidence. The confidence disappeared quickly during the Depression and never came back, outside of a braggadocio which was entirely Celtic and utterly misplaced. The glories of the Victorian stone clad frontages were over, and after the Second World War there were homes to be built for the returning heroes. Before the conflict the city had erected new estates called schemes and had done it very well. Knightswood and Crosspark were noticeable in immediate pre-war Britain. Both were a kind of proletarian Hampstead Garden suburb. Later, towns such as Welwyn Garden City were to emulate the success of the new districts which Glasgow, in its agony of slum land, had decided upon as an amelioration fitting for a new and better world.

But the aftermath of war had left the Second City of Empire with a housing crisis which was met with a half-cocked sort of hysteria. So the solid achievements of the early estates were made positively gelid in the new schemes, with bad planning, bad building, and a wanton disregard for the communities who had toiled so hard during the hard years, and during the War. Easterhouse, Drumchapel, Castlemilk, and many other areas, were thrown up with no sense of community at all. There were no churches or chapels, or schools, or hospitals, or shops, or pubs – and, worst of all, no public transport. Glasgow built its own version of Soweto. Dormitories and worse than dormitories. What Billy Connolly once called "deserts wi' windaes".

Worse than bad planning and bad building was the curious collusion between the complacent bourgeoisie and leftish Glasgow councillors. At one stage a disastrous housing development in Gorbals in which the houses were suffering from the most appalling damp was heavily criticized by the unfortunate tenants. They were told by an especially autocratic councillor, resplendent in his watch chain socialism, that the inhabitants were "breathing too hard". Bad faith. It has marred many an area and has probably been the greatest mistake ever made by any representative ever democratically elected (and Glasgow, we think, is more democratic than anywhere else). But sometimes even democracy does not work and the outlying schemes never really had a chance.

Today the powers that be often inject capital into refurbishment in these estates, but you can tart up the outside as much as you like; the inside is a different matter. If there are no jobs, no work, no continuity from one generation to the other, there will not be a chance for the natives. And the natives will not respond. Recent years have seen a disparity growing in this least disparate of cities. The dispossessed are less obvious but they make up a larger percentage of the population. And the places where the less well off live are ugly, rather uglier than the slums they came from in the great diaspora of the Fifties when there were high hopes for the future. Ugly places make for ugly people and, in common with many another large British city, the outlying districts in Glasgow have produced an underclass which it would seem difficult to counteract.

Yet Glasgow was once a flourishing place and the amazing expansion of it, within a mere century, brought about a quite beautiful city. Colin Baxter came and saw – nobody ever conquers the place – and has caught the activity and vitality, as well as the astonishing liveliness of its architecture. The most famous building in Glasgow is its School of Art designed by Charles Rennie Mackintosh, a famous son (a former pupil of my own school, by the way, which also managed to have as old boys, Lord Melvin, Monty Finnieston, and Ian Hamilton, Q.C., the man who stole the Stone of Destiny, and not bad going that is).

The Glasgow School of Art is a truly astounding building. It rather sums up the Glasgow which Colin took a lens to: Scottish idiosyncratic, a little queer, and, at the end of the day, cheerful. There are many tragedies still, but it remains a city of green tranquillity, with a scarlet dress on it at night, like a lady just a shade past her best, but handsome in the lamplight, a portrait by Whistler in his later days. Trixia in the lamplight is the painting I'm thinking of, still to be seen in the Hunterian Museum of Glasgow University. Sums up Glasgow really. A looker, and good company to boot.

FINNIESTON QUAY CRANE
The highlight of the Clydeside skyline. It is a potent symbol of
Glasgow's industrial decline. No Glaswegian sees the skeletal structure without
a twinge of regret and sentimentality. Opposite: The Waverley is the last working
paddle steamer in the world outside of the tourist areas of the Mississippi.
Greatly loved by Glaswegians, it still goes sedately down the Clyde
and has survived many attempts to kill her off.

THE 'WAVERLEY'

CHARING CROSS

SCOTTISH EXHIBITION & CONFERENCE CENTRE
The Scottish Exhibition Centre has had a variegated
history. It is truly impressive and offers one of the best and largest
venues in Europe for international conferences of any kind.
A focus for Europe it was thought of and
will probably become so.

GLASGOW GARDEN FESTIVAL

Glasgow Garden Festival was not meant to happen.
Glasgow wasn't meant to get it at all. But The Glasgow
Garden Festival in 1988 was more than a triumph: its
success heralded a new Glasgow and led on
to the glory of the city in the
European Year of Culture.

GLASGOW SCHOOL OF ART

Charles Rennie Mackintosh's masterpiece. Mackintosh expressed a kind of
Celtic and romantic yearning in his own version of twentieth-century modernism
and nobody in that century had done it with so much verve, partly because 'Tosh'
belonged to the nineteenth one and was a seer and prophet. He had craftsmanship
as well. Glaswegians have been long in recognising their own and the genius
of Mackintosh was overlooked for over seventy years.

SECOND CITY OF EMPIRE

Across the vista of the West End can be seen the sheer
immensity, scale and confidence of the city as it expanded. The nostalgic
crane recalls a flourishing industrial past which is now lost. But Glasgow
has risen again, and what it will embark upon now will surely
be as romantic, energetic, and as quirkily odd as that which
was started up long years ago.

INDEX OF PLACES